JOHN FIELDER

WASHINGTON

MAGNIFICENT WILDERNESS

PHOTOGRAPHY BY JOHN FIELDER

WESTCLIFFE PUBLISHERS, INC. ENGLEWOOD, COLORADO

CONTENTS

International Standard Book Number:
ISBN 0-942394-21-6
Library of Congress Catalogue Card Number:
86-050063
Copyright, Photographs and Text: John Fielder,
1986
Designer: Gerald Miller Simpson/Denver
Typographer: Edward A. Nies
Printer: Dai Nippon Printing Company, Ltd.,
Tokyo, Japan
Publisher: Westcliffe Publishers, Inc.
Post Office Box 1261
Englewood, Colorado 80150-1261

*First frontispiece: Indian paintbrush and cinquefoil
wildflowers decorate Moraine Park below Willis Wall
and Mt. Rainier, Mt. Rainier National Park*

*Second frontispiece: Sunrise reflects upon Shi-Shi Beach,
Olympic National Park*

*Third frontispiece: Huckleberry, blueberry, and
mountain-ash color the Autumn landscape, Mt. Rainier
National Park*

*Title page: Sea stacks project their image on a beach
made blue by morning light, Point of the Arches,
Olympic National Park*

*Right: Canada mayflower drink the moisture of
frequent coastal rain, near Ruby Beach, Olympic
National Park*

PREFACE

This portfolio of 92 photographs represents my first work in the state of Washington. The images within this book were made over a one year period, during excursions from Colorado of one to six weeks in duration. It was a year of great discovery, for the state provided plants, landforms, and conditions of weather I had never imagined I would see.

I have spent most of my life photographing the alpine domains of Colorado. In 1983 I got the itch to see new places, so I went to California for two years. This period opened my eyes to the diversity of the wilderness world. The ocean, the desert, and hills of oak trees showed me a part of what there was beyond my own Rocky Mountains. Though overwhelmed initially by strange colors and shapes, my California odyssey eventually yielded a large amount of work of which I'm very proud.

Though I continued to photograph Colorado, my curiosity to discover new wrinkles in the crust of our earth led me to the state of Washington. Though I had never been to Washington, impressions had been made on me over the years of a place of great visual drama with a crustal character unique in our country. Faded memories as a child from geology class and transitory glimpses of Washington state in the Rand-McNally atlas formed the fragile foundation for those images in my mind. They were images of Mt. Olympus and Greek gods flying over the peaks, of endless apple orchards and something called the Cascades. From those early years came visions of a peak called Rainier, of infinite forests of cone-bearing trees, and cold

beaches and meandering waterways of the Pacific. My preconceived visual notions of such a land motivated me to go to Washington, but proved to be gross underestimations of the wild beauty that I ultimately found and photographed.

The beginning of my education was very dramatic! My first view of the south side of Mt. Rainier almost sent me off the highway. It was May and I was driving up to Paradise. A trip in April had revealed no peak behind the seemingly permanent clouds, and it appeared that May would hide it, too. As I crossed Kautz Creek, a glacial drain of the nastiest sort, I looked upcreek and there it was — the most awesome looking mountain I had ever seen. My first thought was how much it looked like Everest. I was truly shocked by the ice rolling over its top, of the clouds running past its frigid face. I knew instantly I would be very happy photographing in Washington.

I was also unprepared for the physical task of hauling 75 pounds of camera gear into the Cascades. In Colorado, elevation gains are relatively slow, as trails meander up gentle alluvial plains before opening into alpine basins. In Washington, my first trip into the Alpine Lakes Wilderness showed me how different the geology was between the two mountain ranges. The elevation gains were brutal, and I quickly had thoughts of abandoning half of my lenses and film holders. At 6,000 feet, at tree line, the reward for my effort was plainly apparent. Here was some of the most rugged and precipitous alpine country I had ever seen. Certainly it was as young and unspoiled as any I had explored in

The giants of the beach, like their counterparts the trees
in the nearby forests, dominate the coastal landscape,
Point of the Arches, Olympic National Park

PREFACE

either Colorado or California. The tarns were glacial green, the tundra packed with wildflowers, and the granite peaks simply intimidating. The larch trees along alpine ridges, lime green in spring and brilliant orange in fall, and fleeting glimpses of volcanoes in the distance rejuvenated my spirit and creativity.

I had also underestimated the wildness of the Washington coast. My education here began with three days on Shi-Shi Beach and a week down the North Beach wilderness, both in Olympic National Park. I had expected great beaches of sand, but had never dreamed of beaches of foot-thick polished rocks. The fresh water rills draining down to the ocean, the root tannin stained water that I drank for lunch, and wet forests at beach edge exemplified the character of the Washington coast. Countless starfish clinging to rocks at low tide, whole fields of blue-gray mussels, and the shiny sea water-washed brown algae strewn along the beaches gave me good reason to exceed my photographic film budget. And those giant sea stacks reflecting in tidal pools at sunrise: they must certainly be denizens of some Tibetan plateau transplanted to the shores of Olympia. What a joy it was to discover the magic of tide tables, and their usefulness in avoiding death by drowning while I rounded sea-soaked points of land. I was fascinated with endless forests of supine trees, logging remnants stolen by the Pacific Ocean, choking creeks flowing to the ocean. Thick forests at beach-edge made life saving shelter from wind and rain; how unusual it was to wake up in the morning to the thick saline smell of the sea and its floral denizens, the kelps and algae. This was such a contrast to Colorado's alpine domain.

With the incipient stages of my education about the character of the Washington landscape complete, I moved forward with the business of exploring and photographing the magnificent wilderness of Washington. From early autumn snow storms below Mt. Baker to sunrises of incredible color reflecting on beaches and alpine lakes, I was witness to the dynamic state of weather in the Pacific Northwest. I was even there for the dryest summer in 35 years, a fact that sadly limited my work with wildflowers. The greens of budding alder trees and the flame-reds of autumn's huckleberry and vine maple filled my spirit with the chromatic joy that sometimes eludes me in Colorado and California. From the shapes of century-worn pebbles on the beach to the symmetry of Douglas fir and western cedar trees standing tall across the state, I was overwhelmed by Washington, and truly inspired.

As far as Greek gods are concerned, that was no misconceived notion. It was just as I had imagined. My four day excursion to High Divide overlooking the Hoh River and across to Mt. Olympus was well worth the effort. For on one cold August morning, one half hour before sunrise, I focused on the doric columns of the Pantheon high on the peak. The sun came up and turned white marble to red, and Zeus seemed content as he looked to the Pacific.

John Fielder

For Katy, who was there.

Kalmia wildflowers precede the gaze of Mt. Rainier
upon a fresh water pond, Old Desolate Ridge,
Mt. Rainier National Park

COLOR

"I am stimulated by chromatic diversity in the landscape. Washington exhibits everything from lime-greens of larch trees in Spring to flame-reds of vine maple leaves in Autumn. In essence the camera becomes my paintbrush, the film dyes my oils, and the photographic paper my canvas. Color is an important reason why creating art with a lens is so rewarding to me."

Autumn's vine maple fronts a Ponderosa Pine, along Icicle Creek, Wenatchee National Forest

*Under the summer sun, ice withdraws from an alpine
tarn, Upper Enchantment Basin, Alpine Lakes Wilderness*

*Steam vents from the main crater above the
wasted slopes of Mount St. Helens, Mount St. Helens
National Volcanic Monument*

*Bracken fern glows from the light of storm filtered rays,
along Icicle Creek, Wenatchee National Forest*

*A fresh coating of Pacific waters reflects evening light,
North Wilderness Coast, Olympic National Park*

*Overleaf: Autumn's huckleberry, Paradise Meadow,
Mt. Rainier National Park*

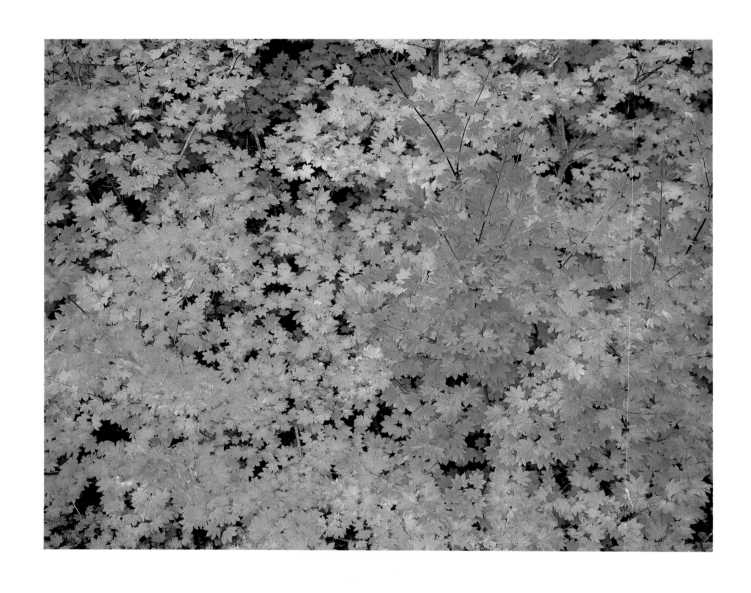

*A contrast of season: Vine maple boasts a spectrum
of color, Autumn, Mt. Rainier National Park;
an alder tree forest manifests the subtlety of Spring,
Mt. Baker-Snoqualmie National Forest*

A vein of milky quartz extrudes from the forest floor;
day-old snow and fallen larch tree needles
compose around dwarf willow leaves, along Cabin Creek,
Alpine Lakes Wilderness

Overleaf: The yellow glow of filtered morning light
envelopes an alpine tarn in tranquility, Old Desolate
Ridge, Mt. Rainier National Park

*A contrast of place: A receding tide exposes rocks
of the marine floor, Point of the Arches, Olympic National
Park; Snow Creek ambles between ancient rocks
of the alpine floor, Upper Enchantment Basin,
Alpine Lakes Wilderness*

Indian paintbrush and lupine, Berkeley Park,
Mt. Rainier National Park

The alpine larch tree and its feathery needles, Autumn,
Cabin Creek drainage, Alpine Lakes Wilderness

A giant cedar peers through the fertile forest,
Mt. Baker-Snoqualmie National Forest

Cottonwood and vine maple trees, along the banks of
the Wenatchee River, Cascade Range

FORM

"Form is not only important to black and white compositions, but to those in color as well. I am particularly stimulated by symmetry in nature, which often is perfect enough so as to appear supernatural. The microcosm of pebbles on the beach, or ferns in the forest, can be as arresting to the eye as any great scenic view. These patterns in nature appear constantly to the vigilant eye."

Sea stacks and pools at low tide compose patterns upon the beach, Point of the Arches, Olympic National Park

*Larch trees and clouds, Cabin Creek drainage,
Alpine Lakes Wilderness*

*Beach pebbles, North Wilderness Coast,
Olympic National Park*

*Morning light: Mountain hemlock atop fractured
rock, Mt. Baker-Snoqualmie National Forest;
weathered driftwood strewn along the beach,
North Wilderness Coast, Olympic National Park*

Driftwood reflects images in fresh water,
North Wilderness Coast, Olympic National Park

Sedimentary rock patterns on the beach, Shi-Shi Beach,
Olympic National Park

Overleaf: Oak ferns make plainly apparent the natural
order on Earth, Mt. Rainier National Park

*Denizens of the forest: Douglas fir and western hemlock
cast shadows on the forest floor, Mt. Rainier National
Park; alder trees cast their shadow on brackish water,
Coal Creek, Olympic National Park*

The surf retreats over polished beach boulders, North Wilderness Coast, Olympic National Park

Larch tree needles compose on ice, Cabin Creek, Alpine Lakes Wilderness

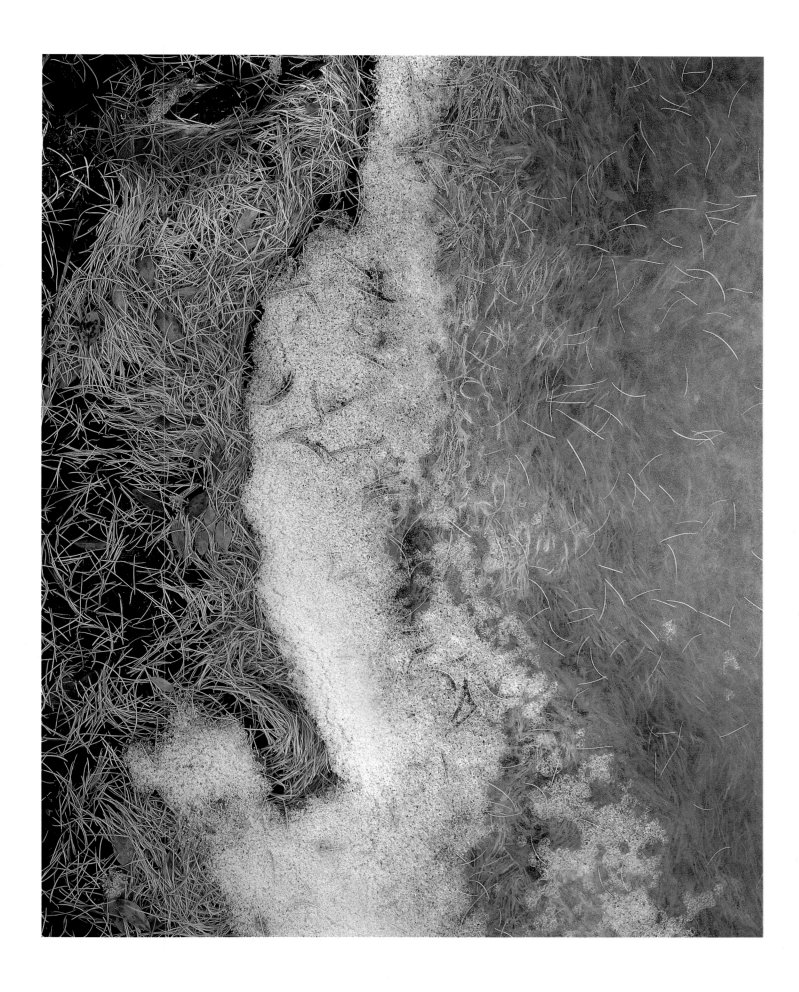

MOMENT

"The quality of light in the natural environment can be as fleeting as the time of day. Red rays from a setting sun and the yellow glow from morning fog can dramatically change the character of the landscape from one moment to the next. These transitory places in time demand the quick reaction of the viewer if he wishes to record them in his memory or upon his film. Therefore, weather and light allow the land to be visually dramatic."

Sunrise upon Little Annapurna Peak — ice recedes from Rune Lake, Lower Enchantment Basin, Alpine Lakes Wilderness

*Storm clouds loom behind cold fir trees of the alpine
domain, Mt. Rainier National Park*

*An Autumn snowfall decorates the edge of Picture Lake,
Heather Meadows, Mt. Baker-Snoqualmie National Forest*

*Overleaf: The blue of the morning sky
reflects onto Shi-Shi Beach, Point of the Arches,
Olympic National Park*

*Sunrise and the Temple from Snow Creek and Upper
Enchantment Basin, Alpine Lakes Wilderness Area*

*Sun rays catch fog above Icicle Creek, Cascade Range,
Wenatchee National Forest*

Morning clouds reflect onto patterns of tidal pools, North Wilderness Coast, Olympic National Park

Martha Falls, along Unicorn Creek, Mt. Rainier National Park

Overleaf: Mt. Rainier projects its north face upon an alpine tarn, from Old Desolate Ridge, Mt. Rainier National Park

Morning showers abate and the clouds retreat:
Cowlitz Chimneys rise above the fog; Goat Island
Mountain looms in the distance, from the Sunrise area,
Mt. Rainier National Park

North Beach Wilderness, from Sand Point,
Olympic National Park

Larch trees drop their needles around Lake Augusta,
Alpine Lakes Wilderness

Overleaf: Tarn and pre-dawn light, Upper Enchantment
Basin, Alpine Lakes Wilderness

Morning rains evaporate and the sun breaks through,
Icicle Creek, Cascade Range

Starfish, Shi-Shi Beach, Olympic National Park

*Evening light: Ice and alpine tarn, Windy Gap,
Mt. Rainier National Park; fading Autumn snowstorm
over Kulshan Ridge, Heather Meadows area,
Mt. Baker-Snoqualmie National Forest*

PLACE

"Certain photographs are constructed in a way that the viewer feels he may be standing behind the photographer. The mechanics of the camera, its depth of focus, allows me to place the viewer into my scene. If I have felt the emotion of that moment in time and that place in nature, the viewer may very well be a real part of the experience, too.

Martha Falls plunges into Unicorn Creek, Mt. Rainier National Park

Douglas fir and western hemlock,
southern Cascade Range

Lupine drink from Lodi Creek, Berkeley Park,
Mt. Rainier National Park

Overleaf: Sunset, Point of the Arches,
Olympic National Park

*Motion and repose: Matheny Creek rushes
towards the Queets River, in the rain forest, Olympic
National Park; cottonwood leaves rest beside the
Wenatchee River, Cascade Range*

Morning light in the rain forest, above the Quinault River,
Olympic National Forest

Freshly fallen snow on mountain-ash and willows,
Heather Meadows, Mt. Baker-Snoqualmie National Forest

Overleaf: Sandless beach, North Wilderness Coast,
Olympic National Park

Clearing storm, Highwood Lake in Heather Meadows,
Mt. Baker-Snoqualmie National Forest

Falls, along the Soleduck River, Olympic National Park

No Name Creek, Mt. Adams Wilderness
Vine maple, Autumn, Gifford Pinchot National Forest

*A contrast of season: Ponds in Autumn, at the
headwaters of Cabin Creek; scouring-rush in Spring,
along Snow Creek, Alpine Lakes Wilderness*

Sword ferns in the rain forest, Queets River,
Olympic National Park

Lodi Creek, Berkeley Park, Mt. Rainier National Park

Overleaf: The low morning sun illuminates green algae,
North Wilderness Coast, Olympic National Park

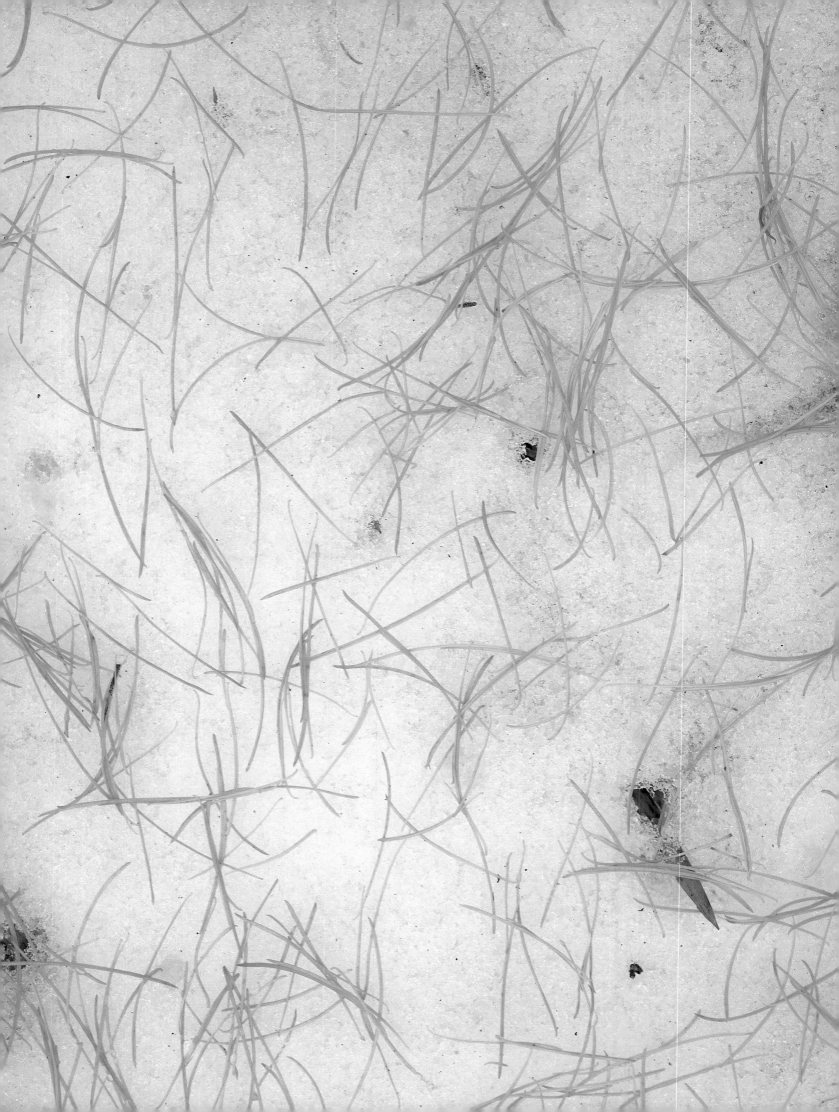

INFINITY &
MICROCOSM

"Images of very small parts of the landscape may be as arresting as those of sky and earth. The shapes and colors that occur beneath our feet are trodden upon and overlooked by the most observant of wilderness visitors. Conversely, we sometimes fail to perceive those dramatic meetings of sky and earth. I try to maximize my wilderness experience by observing all of nature's dimensions."

Larch tree needles on snow, beside Lake Augusta, Alpine Lakes Wilderness

Similitude of color: Evening light, North Wilderness Coast; mussel shells, Shi-Shi Beach, Olympic National Park

Overleaf: Tarn and morning light, Upper Enchantment Basin, Alpine Lakes Wilderness

Icicle Ridge, Alpine Lakes Wilderness
Cedar bark, Berkeley Park, Mt. Rainier National Park

*Macrocosm and microcosm: surf-pounded formations and
brown algae, Shi-Shi Beach, Olympic National Park*

*Ice finally recedes from one of the Upper Enchantment
Lakes, Alpine Lakes Wilderness*

*A thicket of wild parsley, Seven Lakes Basin,
Olympic National Park*

The Puyallup River and Mt. Rainier,
Mt. Rainier National Park

Wood sorrel contrast against rain-soaked maple leaves,
Olympic National Forest

Overleaf: An area no larger than one half
of a foot square reveals the shapes and colors of the
North Wilderness Coast, Olympic National Park

*Mt. Fitzhenry and Mt. Carrie loom high over the rugged
ridges of the Olympic Range, Olympic National Park*

Mussels, Shi-Shi Beach, Olympic National Park

The warm summer sun consumes the last of the ice on Upper Enchantment Lakes, Alpine Lakes Wilderness

A close look reveals nature's own symmetry on the North Wilderness Coast, Olympic National Park

Overleaf: Autumn snowstorm, Austin Pass, Heather Meadows area, Mt. Baker-Snoqualmie National Forest

TECHNICAL
INFORMATION

The images within this book were made with a Linhof Super Technika 4″ × 5″ field view camera. Lenses of 75mm, 115mm, 150mm, 210mm, 300mm, 360mm, and 500mm were used.

Ektachrome 64 daylight transparency film was used exclusively. Yellow color correcting filters were used to correct for the cyan imbalance in the film. Ultraviolet and polarizing filters were also used on occasion.

Exposures were calculated with a Pentax 1° digital Spot Meter using both a gray card and values of light reflecting from the landscape. Exposures varied from 1/60 second to 40 seconds. Apertures ranged from f4.5 to f64.

Reproduction of the images on this paper was done with the aid of state of the art laser scanning machines, and with the intention of duplicating the view as it appeared to the naked eye.

Cabin Creek Basin displays the last of its Autumn Color, Alpine Lakes Wilderness